I AM 99

A Southern Resident Orca Story

By Keri Newman

Illustrated by Ashton Alba

I Am 99: A Southern Resident Orca Story. Copyright © 2021 Keri Newman. Produced and printed by Stillwater River Publications. All rights reserved. Written and produced in the United States of America. This book may not be reproduced or sold in any form without the expressed, written permission of the authors and publisher.

Visit our website at **www.StillwaterPress.com** for more information.

First Stillwater River Publications Edition

Library of Congress Control Number: 2021904453

ISBN: 978-1-952521-95-9

1 2 3 4 5 6 7 8 9 10

Written by Keri Newman
Illustrated by Ashton Alba
Published by Stillwater River Publications, Pawtucket, RI, USA.

Publisher's Cataloging-In-Publication Data
(Prepared by The Donohue Group, Inc.)

Names: Newman, Keri, author. | Alba, Ashton, illustrator.
Title: I am 99 : a southern resident orca story / by Keri Newman ; illustrated by Ashton Alba.
Description: First Stillwater River Publications edition. | Pawtucket, RI, USA : Stillwater River Publications, [2021] | Interest age level: 005-009. | Summary: "Sailor-Lyn wants to learn all she can about the southern resident orcas she sees in Friday Harbor. When she finds out there are only 72 whales left, she makes a promise to help save them from extinction. Will there be 99 whales again … or will something even better happen?"--Provided by publisher.
Identifiers: ISBN 9781952521959
Subjects: LCSH: Killer whale--Conservation--Washington (State)--Friday Harbor--Juvenile fiction. | Endangered species--Washington (State)--Friday Harbor--Juvenile fiction. | Sailors--Washington (State)--Friday Harbor--Juvenile fiction. | CYAC: Killer whale--Conservation--Washington (State)--Friday Harbor--Fiction. | Endangered species--Washington (State)--Friday Harbor--Fiction. | Sailors--Washington (State)--Friday Harbor--Fiction.
Classification: LCC PZ7.1.N4858 Ia 2021 | DDC [Fic]--dc23

The views and opinions expressed in this book are solely those of the author and do not necessarily reflect the views and opinions of the publisher.

Dedicated to children everywhere
who help protect our ocean friends.

Dedicated to you.

To Paisley

Sailor-Lyn didn't know many people when her family moved to the small town of Friday Harbor. She passed the time by running errands with her mother and watching the boats and seaplanes come in and out of the marina.

Her favorite place to spend the long August days, however, was a place called Lime Kiln State Park. Sailor-Lyn would carefully walk the rocky paths toward the lighthouse and find a private spot on the rocks to look out at the Pacific Ocean.

Some days she would sit there for hours and see nothing but the waves and an occasional seal. On special days, she would see the fins of killer whales, far off in the distance.

On VERY special days, she would see the whales come much closer! Sailor-Lyn was mesmerized by these beautiful animals. She wanted to learn everything she could about them.

On August 12, Sailor-Lyn woke up extra early. It was her birthday. She had asked for a whale journal so she could keep track of everything she saw. She couldn't wait to open her presents and head to the lighthouse.

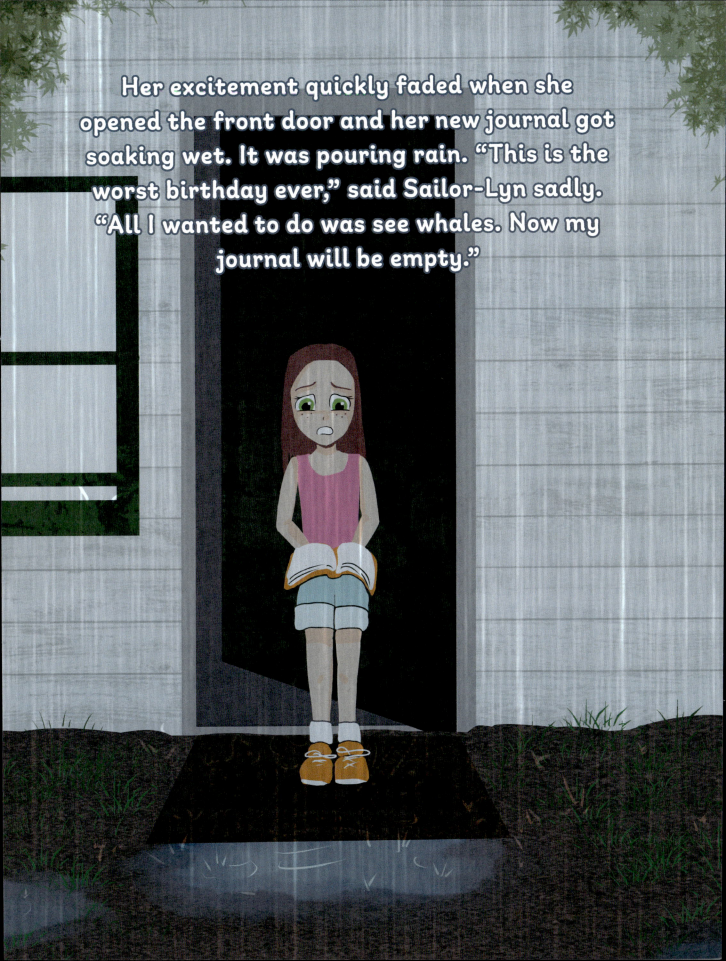

But Sailor-Lyn's mother had an idea.
"We are going to a little place that I think
you may like," she said with a sly smile.
"Bring that journal with you."

Sailor-Lyn met Captain Ben, a marine biologist who had been studying whales for over 40 years. He showed Sailor-Lyn the many journals they had of killer whales. She couldn't believe her eyes.

"Would you like to join our crew on the water tomorrow?" Ben asked an excited Sailor-Lyn.

The next morning, the crew and Sailor-Lyn boarded a small boat and headed out to sea. "The killer whales you've been seeing around here are called *Southern Resident Orcas*," Ben explained. "They live in three families called pods. There is J Pod, K Pod, and L Pod."

J POD

"I wish that were true," said Ben. "You see, they are almost extinct. If we don't do something to help them quickly, there won't be any left." Sailor-Lyn couldn't imagine a world without these beautiful animals she had come to love so much.

K POD

Ben sighed. "They don't have enough food to eat. You see, these Southern Resident Orcas don't eat seals or sea lions like a lot of other killer whales do. They eat Chinook salmon. And there's not a lot of salmon left out here."

L POD

Ben could see that Sailor-Lyn was sad.
"I have been studying this group for a long time. At one time, there were 99 orcas. Today, there are only 72. We can help them," he continued, "but it will take a lot of hard work."

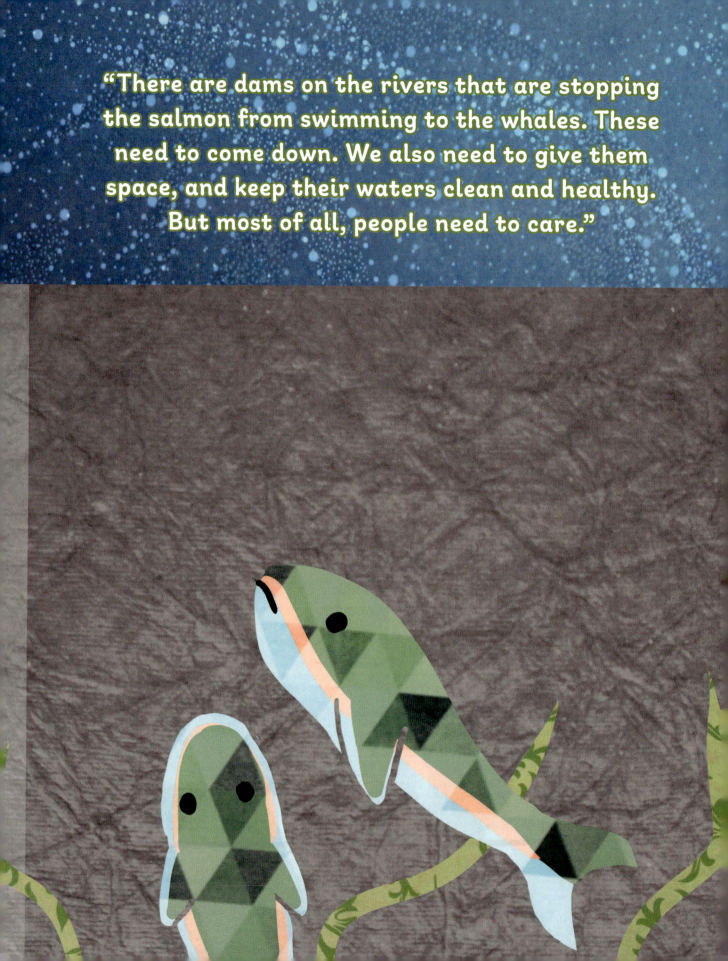

"There are dams on the rivers that are stopping the salmon from swimming to the whales. These need to come down. We also need to give them space, and keep their waters clean and healthy. But most of all, people need to care."

Sailor-Lyn was determined to keep that promise. She went straight home and started a petition to save the Southern Resident Orcas.

Sailor-Lyn told everyone she knew about Southern Resident Orcas needing salmon and asked everyone to sign her petition. She met many new people and made many new friends. She worked... day after day... year after year.

Until one day it was time for her to leave the island
she loved to go study whales across the country.
She promised her friends she would return.

Four years went by, and Sailor-Lyn did come back to Friday Harbor. She came back on the very best day ever! For when she looked out at the ocean, she saw a little black and white head pop out of the water.

Sailor-Lyn jumped for joy! Because of her and all of the friends that she made, there were finally 99 Southern Resident Orcas again. This called for a celebration!

The town all gathered for a big parade.
And 99 was a celebrity!

When the celebration winded down, Sailor-Lyn went out to her favorite rock at Lime Kiln State Park and took out her old whale journal. What a perfect entry this would be. What could possibly be better?

TAKE THE 99 PLEDGE TO SAVE THE WHALES!

The Southern Resident Orcas will go extinct without your help.

You can make a difference by taking the "99 Pledge" and sharing with your friends. You can be a Whale Hero.

- I will be heard! I will talk to people about helping whales get the salmon they need to eat.
- I will keep the ocean clean.
- I will pick up litter, recycle, and reuse all that I can.
- I will care enough to share the story of southern resident orcas with others.
- I will make a difference so that one day there will be 99 (and more) Southern Resident Orcas.
- I will be a Whale Hero!

....
Signature   Date

This Certificate recognizes that

_____

has taken the 99 Pledge to save the Southern Resident Orcas and is a Whale Hero.

Twisted Orca

Date:

ABOUT THE AUTHOR

Keri Newman is a Marine Naturalist and member of the Salish Sea Association of Marine Naturalists. She graduated from the University of Rhode Island with a degree in English and Communications. She fell in love with killer whales when she was three years old, and she has been passionate about marine conservation ever since.

ABOUT THE ILLUSTRATOR

Ashton Alba is an artist and illustrator currently living in Florida. Her art has been displayed in businesses, galleries, and museums across the country. She holds a Scholastic Silver Key in story board art, four congressional citations for artistic excellence, and numerous awards in art and photography.

Twisted Orca's mission is to foster a love of marine life and inspire future generations of marine conservationists. Every child should have the opportunity to fall in love with marine life!

Collect the entire fun and educational series!

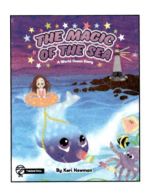 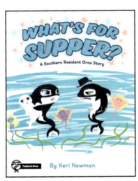 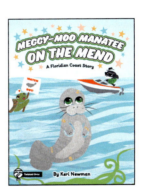

 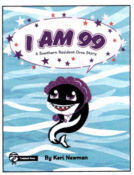

For more marine life information, fun, and ways to help, visit us online at:

WWW.TWISTEDORCA.COM

Made in the USA
Monee, IL
30 March 2021